Table of Contents

When the Midnight Stars

When the midnight stars

fell to earth

And the god rays lose

their luster

When the Sun, dim,

leaves a cracked hearth

And the spring dew leaves

dried grass in a cluster

When the dynamic beauty

of nature retreats

And the excitement gives

way to lethargy

Find me adrift in

a waveless sea

Alone, eternal, and

content to be

The Bustle of the City

The bustle of the city

lives on in my brain

The clatter of the metro

and shattered window panes

Will always remind me of

turn dials and trains

Of large analogue clocks

and colorful aeroplanes

Of murmuring crowds and

crooked lanes

Under a canopy of trees

in a grassy plain

I smile and remember that the bustle

of the city lives on in my brain

What Madness Wrought

What madness wrought

the clashing keys

That brought baroque

to its knees

What inspired entropic mask

born of that hectic dance

Gave way and charge

to the violet lance

Guided by piano tones

and the creatures unknown to roam

Bottled all of creation in a flask

buried and hidden in loam

Fill the Void

Fill the void

they said with glee

Fill it with

cheerful misery

Fill it so

it continues to grow

Fill it and

hope the rot slows

Fill it until

it bursts and spills

Fill it to

drown out the ill

Fill it and

breathe, try not to scream

Fill it and

remember to support the team

Fill it quickly

never failing

Fill it as

you're swiftly ailing

Fill the bottomless

void in your soul

Fill the void

forevermore

I Want to Go Somewhere

I want to go Somewhere

where dreams come true

out of reach except for You

I want to go Somewhere

where I can rest

fully beyond the grip of the test

I want to go Somewhere

and maybe somewhen

where I can see what happens Then

Then, they say, "Remember when

she walked and talked with us?

Remember her laugh, so boisterous?

Remember her wit and her smile?

Remember her tears that flowed for miles?

Remember how we loved her so?

Remember how she'll never know?

Remember when we asked her to stay?

Remember when she went anyway?

Somewhere is lonely and oh so cold

and Then it leaks into the fold

But Then never has to be

as long as Somewhere I never see

Sing a Sad Song for Me

Sing a sad song for me
with an upbeat tune
Drown out the words
with a rhythmic beat
Sing it so they can see
and grant me the boon
Of listening so that I am heard
and drawing near to take a seat

Sing a happy song for me
that cries smooth and slow
Whose tones draw tears to the eyes
and threaten to bring unease
Sing it so that I can be free
from the chains that keep me low
Free of the hidden pain and public lies
sing so that it will cease

Sing of me and my disguise
mirror my path with song
Sing to show the depth of my cries
And my life, so long
Sing of me and I'll sing of you
for I know you feel it to

You Can Find Me by the Sea

You can find me by the sea
waiting to be
foam on the waves
everyday

Look for me in the reeds
neglecting my needs
wasting away
day by day

Resting on the sand
heart in my hand
ashes and clay
one day

Buried in the mud
left by the flood
or adrift in the bay
someday

Wishing for the rust
bones to dust
slowly decay
yesterday

Feet firmly on the ground
no waves to be found
making a way
today

I Don't Want to Leave

I don't want to leave

but I can't bear to stay

I don't want to part

but I'm drifting away

I'm trying to hold on tight

but it's hard not to let go

I'm trying to win the fight

but I'm losing my head

I want to stand firm

but I am of two minds

I want to believe

but faith is hard to find

I might feel alone

but You are always here

I might be on my own

but Your help is always near

I still don't want to leave

but I know it's for the best

I still don't know what's next

but I'll stand the test

I can't help but wait

but I want to look ahead

I can't help but be great

but not without You

Dread the Day and the Night

Dread the day and the night
Dread the march but still fight
To keep yourself above the mire
To emerge unscathed from the fire
Fall but do not fail to rise
Keep your gaze upon the prize
And when this time comes to an end
You will have a chance to mend
As a soldier, proud and true
The Army's ranks accepting you
So, stand strong through Nature's rages
Keep marching though it's felt like ages
And four days hence you will believe
The worth of the work as the reward you receive

I Cannot See the Path

I cannot see the path
yet my feet fall sure
for my gaze is level upon my Lord.

Though fires rage and waters rise
my heart stays fixed upon His Word.

Through darkened valleys and perilous cliffs
His grace and mercy are a tethering cord.

My life is upheaved and my future uncertain
Yet by His promise my place is assured.

To Walk in Darkness

To walk in darkness
while seeking the light
To carry the burden
and continue the fight
To wander in shadows
of emotions contrite
To pick up the pace
growing in might
To step out in faith
not seeing the path
To keep moving forward
no matter the math
To carve out joy
in a crude swath
To find it's alright
And rest at last

A Thornbush of Roses

A thornbush of roses
A sparrow-less tree
A basket made empty
This is me

A burning husk
A door hanging free
An uneven pathway
This is me

A meal abandoned
A cold black tea
A house with no entrance
This is me

I am a promise for beauty untold
I am a work progressing evermore
I am a treasure hidden in view
A contradiction at the core
This is me

Dear Me, Myself, and I

Dear Me, Myself, and I,

I can't help but lie and tell you it's all fine. To Me, I say that we've been freed and it's okay to be ourselves. To Myself, I say that we've been taken off the shelf and our potential is limitless and we grow in internal wealth. To I, it seems that you know the truth. We're broken and bleeding and always we cry. We fight and fall, rise and fail. Yet through it all hope prevails.

Hope! What a burden to weigh down our soul. It boosts the spirits that reality stole but the day must come when hope lays smashed and we are left churning in a tightening cask.

Ah I, what to say that will put you at ease, that will lighten your pathway and give you the means to make our lies true and make life less cruel. Alas, I haven't the words to set such a scene. Turn not to me, but to letters written in ages past, the scene was cast, and bound in a book. Translated for centuries, eventually it came to our hands. Here it lands.

So, it stands that we must read this book. Take a look, all the answers we seek are inside. We just have to find the page where a loving voice says, "Dear You".

The Reaches of Space

The reaches of space
Are monotonous
And yet incessant

This Place Makes Me Puke

This place makes me puke
In a crimson hued spectrum
Through rigid dry lips

It's Said That Beauty Rests in the Beholder's Eye

It's said that beauty rests in the beholder's eye
So, look at the division in my heart and sigh
At the wonderous collection of guilt and lies
And gaze upon the fractions of my soul and cry
At the gorgeous reflection of all the failed tries
Admire the scars of my being and wonder why
With all the broken and missing pieces, I've not died
Worry not, my end is nigh

Golden Goblets and Brass Gongs

Golden goblets and brass gongs
Crashing silent in dining halls
Crystal vases and glass songs
Shatter and harsh answer the call
Marble memories and pearl tongs
Lay cracked in dust against the wall
Silken blinds and velvet wrongs
Heap unraveled as they fall

Perched On a Bright Star

Perched on a bright star
The dragon waits claws open
An astral meal nears

Search For Me

Search for me
for I can't find myself
Seek me out
like a lost treasure
And if by and by
you happen to find
The reason for
my being
Bury it deep
hide it from me
And cover your trail
behind you

Don't Bank the Fires

Don't bank the fires
of my soul
For we are but embers
in the coal
Should you bury us
in the shoals
Or perchance cover us
with a bowl
We would perish and
pay the toll
Without even smoke to show
we played our role

Witness the Shine

Witness the shine
of a star rising from the brine
Witness the leap
of hope escaping the keep
Witness the audacity
as my dreams shift into reality
Witness it all
and watch me rise from the fall

Forget Me Not

Forget me not
When I am gone
Please keep me in thought
Though the journey is long
Just give it a shot
Maybe it's wrong
To request a gift unbought
But if you hear this song
Please forget me not

In the Winter I dream of the Ocean

In the winter I dream of the ocean
Locked in an airtight cityscape it gives me the notion
That sunlight is near and open skies with clouds in motion
I'd be there now if not for duty and devotion
Hence my emotion

It's a Laughable Scene

It's a laughable scene
Through crimson means
The mellow was shattered like a crystal dream
Like wine spilled and deemed
Unworthy

Blissful Blisters Remind Me That I Am Not Undone

Blissful blisters remind me that I am not undone
Timely echoes of tragedies when I wasn't overcome
Peaceful pains remind me that my race is run
Gathered aches of challenges of which I am the sum

Peaceful Farms Are All Consumed

Peaceful farms are all consumed
By relationships exhumed
In pumpkin patches and in the town
Paramours are left jilted and down
The orchard hides a pair of trees
In the likeness of the thieves
That attempted to steal the farmer's wife
In return he took their life
Take note my novice friend
In this valley we all defend
So, take care when you make your choices
For in these hills, we all have voices

When Emotions Inchoate Inhabit the Soul

When emotions inchoate inhabit the soul
When the heart lies heavy and lethargic and
darker than coal
When the being is writhing and diseased and
riddled with coils
Of envy and hatred and motives unbound
The actions taken will become unsound
And thus begins another round
When the victor, jubilant, emerges from the pit
His foe, conniving, is left to sit
Stewing in wonderings for mankind not fit
Soon emotions begin to take hold
And the heart lies heavy encased in mold
And the being takes action unfit to be told
And the round begins and 'round it goes
And emotions inchoate inhabit the soul

The Monotonous Drone

The monotonous drone
The incessant whine
All drive to insanity
This friend of mine
The partners inept
The roommates unkempt
All cast his mind from its solemn reign
Thrown from a marble parapet all that remains
Are the fevered musings of when and doom
Worry not your time comes soon

Drift With Me in the Way of the Condemned

Drift with me in the way of the condemned
Tired and unresting and sleeping they send
This message to those whom they hope to mend:

To all who walk the paths of life to the end
Take caution against what resources you spend
For this is with what we must contend –
The monotonous reaches of time unending,
The incessant breaches of voids eternally pending,
The insane niches of space twisting and bending,
But take caution not to rend
That on which you must depend
For with it you will defend
All that to which you tend

I Have Purposed in My Heart

I have purposed in my heart
that I will never fall apart
I will always give my all
I will ever answer the call
My strength will grow like a cancer
rapid and vast when given the chance to

I have purposed in my soul
that where You send me, I will go
To the oceans, though I have no gills
To the poles, though I fear the chill
To destinations both far and near
I will travel within Your care

I've Jumped the Tower and Lasted the Chamber

I've jumped the tower and lasted the chamber
Rucked for miles and still I'm unable
To overcome the hardest part
I'd rather plot on a Land Nav chart
But now I start
To undertake the task
Difficult to master yet harder to mask
How to begin a journey so strange
That when complete the whole world will change
To find a gift not found on a shelf
To find a way to love myself

Start the Fires of My Joy

Start the fires of my joy
With kindling wept with weeping
Stoke the flames as they dim
With barbs and careless murmuring
When they fade, please marvel at
The weakness of my embers
And when they've gone, take wonder at
The bleak chill of the ashes
When my soul's grown cold
From lack of warmth
Chastise me for my transgressions
For had I not wept or taken heed
Surely the fires would have been tended

My Mistake was that I Wept

My mistake was that I wept
But for that, I would be kept
From the cliff I should have leapt
At least then I could have slept

Would That I

Would that I
Could write a word
To lift my soul
From weeping

Yet here I sigh
Nothing heard
Attempting to play a role
Uncertain if it's worth keeping

Why should I cry
And not sing as a bird
With no need to cajole
And a heart full to heaping

Sometimes It's Fit

Sometimes it's fit
Merely to sit
And watch the world pass by
At times like this
I live to exist
And leave all to Him on high

Brought Up from a Low Place

Brought up from a low place
I've been restored
By messengers sent
from my Lord
He saw my pain
and sent a balm
Soothed my aches
and gave me calm
To face the rigors
of the test
Promising soon
I will see rest

I Walk by Myself

I walk by myself
Shielded by Your grace and love
And so not alone

I Am Faint

I am faint
For the weight of hope
Hold it that I may rest
Take caution that
It doesn't grow
And crush you flat beneath it

What to Sing

What to sing
        to lift me up
                and leave the clouds behind me
What to write
        to ease my heart
                and erase the pain inside me
What to draw
        to light my soul
                and deny those that despise me
What to read
        to dry my tears
                and walk with joy beside me
How to craft
        anything
                to change the world that surrounds me
You, oh Lord,
        are the key
                to all that confounds me

I Ask the Wind

I ask the wind
To ignore the trees
And blow the sunlight to me
I desire the warmth
Though inside I know
It's never meant to be
I ask anyway
And inside I say
Of my Lord, wait and see

I Find Me in the Winds

I find me in the winds
Cast about on angry waves
I lost me in the fields
Hidden by generous grains
I called You as I sank
In violent skyward storms
I sat silent as I ate
Of the bounty surrounding me

I Miss the Me

I miss the me
I used to be
I've lost the me
I dreamt to see
I've no idea of the me
That can be free

I've Lost My Smile

I've lost my smile
And wear only a likeness
Dim is the light in my eyes
Now a glassy reflection
The curl of my lip
Can now measure a line
The wrinkle in my brow
Has been ironed smooth